Animals in Danger in Africa

Louise and Richard Spilsbury

Heinemann
LIBRARY
Chicago, Illinois

Edited by Rebecca Rissman, Dan Nunn, and Adrian Vigliano
Designed by Philippa Jenkins
Picture research by Tracy Cummins
Originated by Capstone Global Library Ltd.
Printed in China by South China Printing Company, Ltd.

17 16 15 14 13
10 9 8 7 6 5 4 3 2 1

Library of Congress Cataloging-in-Publication Data
Cataloging-in-Publication data is on file at the Library of Congress.
ISBN: 978-1-4329-7672-9 (HC) 978-1-4329-7679-8 (PB)

Acknowledgments
The author and publisher are grateful to the following for permission to reproduce copyright material: Arkive p. 9 (© Philippe Geniez); Biosphoto p. 23 (© Gilles Martin); Corbis pp. 13 (© Ingo Arndt/Minden Pictures), 14 (© Joe McDonald); FLPA pp. 22 (David Hosking), 26 (Michael Gore); Getty Images pp. 18 (Winfried Wisniewski), 25 (Martin Harvey); istockphoto p. 17 (© Peter Malsbury); National Geographic Stock p. 21 (PETE OXFORD/MINDEN PICTURES); Newscom pp. 28 (GREEN RENAISSANCE/ www.greenrenaissance.co.za / HANDOUT/EPA), 29 (David de la Paz/Xinhua/Sipa Pres); Photo Researchers, Inc. p. 11 (© Michel & Christine Denis-Huot); Shutterstock pp. 4 (© Chris P.), 5 bottom (© Rechitan Sorin), 5 top (© Trombax), 6 (© Christopher Poe), 10 (© Sergey Khachatryan), 19 (© PRILL), 27 (© Arnold John Labrentz), icons (© Florian Augustin), (© tristan tan), maps (© AridOcean); Superstock p. 15 (© Minden Pictures).

Cover photograph of an African plain in Kenya produced with permission of Shutterstock (© meunierd).
Cover photograph of golden-crowned sifaka reproduced with permission of SuperStock (© NHPA).
Cover photograph of a white Egyptian vulture reproduced with permission of Shutterstock (© r.martens).
Cover photograph of a male silverback gorilla reproduced with permission of Shutterstock (© Mike Price).
Cover photograph of a black rhinoceros mother with calf reproduced with permission of Superstock (© Minden Pictures).

We would like to thank Michael Bright for his invaluable help in the preparation of this book.

Every effort has been made to contact copyright holders of any material reproduced in this book. Any omissions will be rectified in subsequent printings if notice is given to the publisher.

All the Internet addresses (URLs) given in this book were valid at the time of going to press. However, due to the dynamic nature of the Internet, some addresses may have changed, or sites may have changed or ceased to exist since publication. While the author and publisher regret any inconvenience this may cause readers, no responsibility for any such changes can be accepted by either the author or the publisher.

Contents

Some words are shown in bold, **like this.** You can find out what they mean by looking in the glossary.

Where Is Africa?

We divide the world into seven large areas of land called **continents**. Africa is the second-biggest continent in the world. It covers about one-fifth of the total land area on Earth!

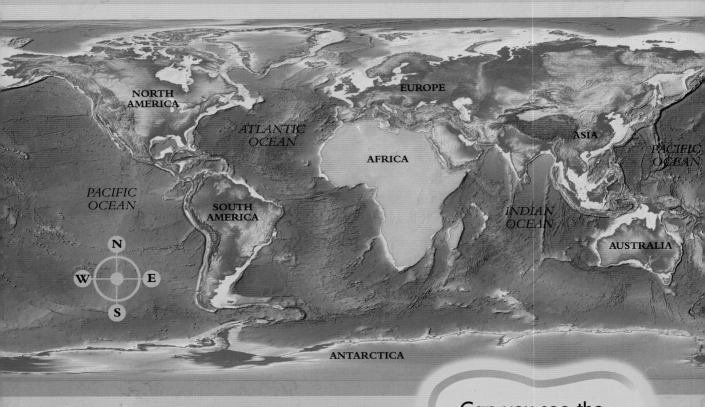

NORTH AMERICA

EUROPE

ASIA

ATLANTIC OCEAN

AFRICA

PACIFIC OCEAN

PACIFIC OCEAN

SOUTH AMERICA

INDIAN OCEAN

AUSTRALIA

N
W   E
S

ANTARCTICA

Can you see the continent of Africa?

Africa is huge, so there are many different kinds of wild places here. There are wide sandy **deserts**, islands, tall forests, and flat **grasslands**. Many animals live in these different **habitats**.

grassland

It is hot and sunny in most parts of Africa.

desert

Animals of Africa

Some animals in Africa are **endangered**. This means there are very few of that type of animal left. If they all die, that type of animal will be **extinct**. An animal that is extinct is gone from the planet forever!

Mandrills might be endangered soon, because people cut down the forests they live in.

Different types of animals look and behave differently from each other. We sort them into groups to help tell them apart.

Animal Classification Chart

Amphibian	• lives on land and in water • has damp, smooth skin • has **webbed** feet • lays many eggs	
Bird	• has feathers and wings • hatches out of hard-shelled eggs	
Fish	• lives in water • has **fins** and most have **scales** • young hatch from soft eggs	
Mammal	• drinks milk when a baby • has hair on its body	
Reptile	• has scales on its body • lives on land • young hatch from soft-shelled eggs	

Look out for pictures like these next to each photo. They will tell you what type of animal each photo shows.

North Africa

In the north there are **deserts** and areas of dry land with few plants. People cut down many trees for fires here. They take over land for farming. **Global warming** dries land and kills plants, too.

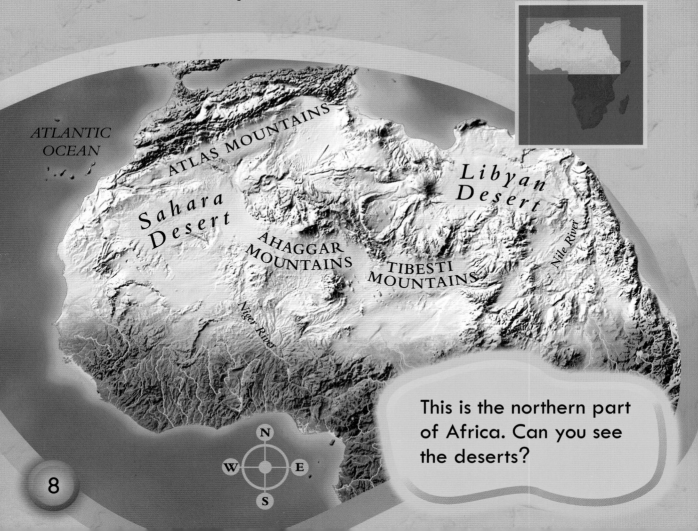

ATLANTIC OCEAN

ATLAS MOUNTAINS

Sahara Desert

AHAGGAR MOUNTAINS

TIBESTI MOUNTAINS

Libyan Desert

Nile River

Niger River

This is the northern part of Africa. Can you see the deserts?

The two fingered skink is a thin, worm-like lizard. It hunts **insects** and other small animals. It has four tiny legs that help it dig burrows under the sand, where it hides from the heat and from **predators**.

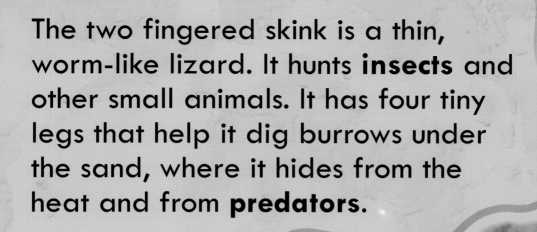

Today there are fewer skinks because there is less land where they can live and feed.

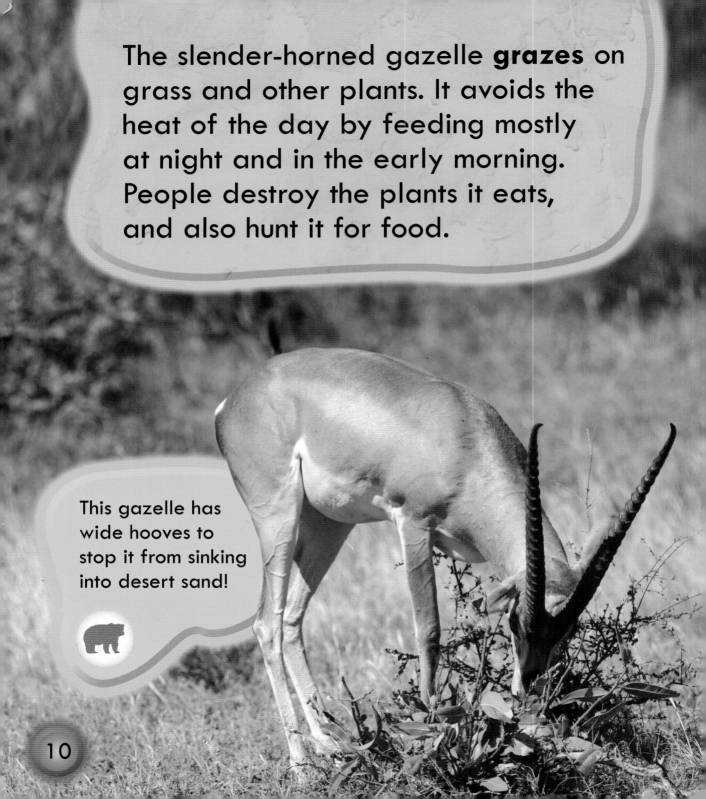

The slender-horned gazelle **grazes** on grass and other plants. It avoids the heat of the day by feeding mostly at night and in the early morning. People destroy the plants it eats, and also hunt it for food.

This gazelle has wide hooves to stop it from sinking into desert sand!

The Egyptian vulture throws stones at eggs to break open their shells!

The Egyptian vulture flies across open land looking for dead animals. It eats dead grazing animals, such as deer. The Egyptian vulture also eats birds' eggs. Fewer plants mean fewer grazing animals for vultures to eat.

Central and West Africa

Some animals are **endangered** in Central and West Africa because people cut down **rain forest** trees to build homes and farms and to sell the wood. People hunt animals for food or even to sell as pets.

Niger River

Rain Forest

Mount Cameroon

Congo River

Equator

N
W E
S

This map shows rain forests in Central and West Africa.

Chimpanzees need rain forests to survive. They eat fruit, leaves, and **insects** found in the forest. They use their long arms and strong fingers to swing through trees to find food.

At night, chimps sleep in treetop nests, where they are safe from **predators**.

Dwarf crocodiles hunt for fish and small animals in rain forest pools or rivers. They build nests from leaves that give off heat as they rot. This keeps crocodile eggs warm, so the babies inside can grow!

A dwarf crocodile protects its eggs and the babies that hatch from them.

A large male gorilla looks fearsome, but he rarely has to fight!

Gorillas walk a long way each day, finding fruit and leaves to eat. They live in groups of females and young, led by a male. He scares off other males by roaring, ripping branches, and beating his chest!

15

East Africa

In East Africa, there are **grasslands**, lakes, and **wetlands**. People clear grasslands and drain wetlands to build homes and ranches. Wide, open spaces that many animals need to survive are now broken up by fences.

Can you see lakes and grasslands on this map of East Africa?

Nile River

Mount Kenya

Equator

Mount Kilimanjaro

Lake Victoria

Lake Tanganyika

Lake Malawi

Grassland

GREAT RIFT VALLEY

N
W E
S

The African wild dog's huge ears help it hear other dogs far across the grassland.

African wild dogs need wide, open spaces. They work in packs to catch big **grazing** animals such as antelopes. Some dogs chase **prey** a long way toward other dogs in their pack that are waiting to catch it!

A cheetah hunts alone. It can sneak up on prey because the color of its fur and its spotted markings help it to blend in with tall grass. Then it races forward to grab grazing animals like gazelles.

The cheetah is the fastest sprinter in the animal world!

The shoebill's beak is about 8 inches (20 centimeters) long!

The shoebill has a huge, shoe-shaped beak. It stands very still in muddy wetlands, watching for prey. Then it quickly grabs and crushes fish, frogs, and other animals in its powerful beak.

19

African Islands

Many animals on islands are **endangered** because people burn trees to clear land for farms, homes, and tourist hotels. People also cut trees for wood and fires and sometimes hunt animals for food.

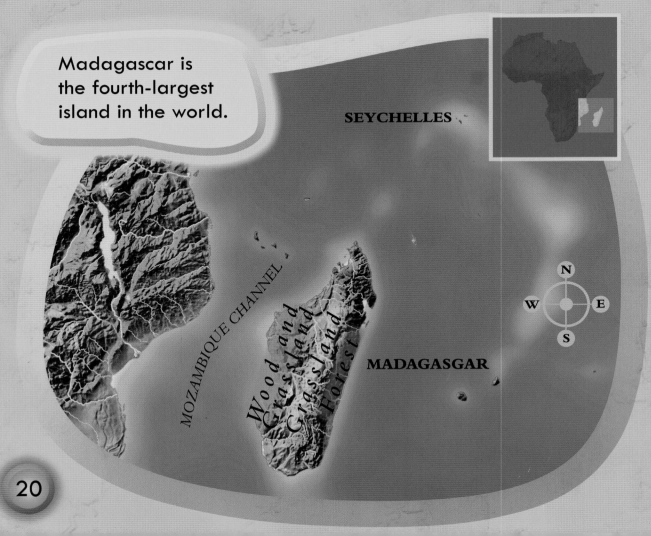

Madagascar is the fourth-largest island in the world.

SEYCHELLES

MOZAMBIQUE CHANNEL

Wood and Grassland

Grassland

Forest

MADAGASGAR

N
W   E
S

The Western woolly lemur carries its young through the trees.

There are 100 types of lemurs. All live only on Madagascar and many are endangered. The Western woolly lemur sleeps in trees in the day. At night, it leaps through trees, looking for leaves to eat.

21

The Gardiner's tree frog is just a centimeter long—not much bigger than your fingernail.

The tiny Gardiner's tree frog lives only on the Seychelles islands. It hunts tiny animals like mites at night, and its colors help it to hide among leaves in the day. Sticky pads on its feet help it to cling to trees!

The tiger chameleon lives in trees on the Seychelles islands, too. Its long tongue rolls up inside its mouth. Then the tongue shoots out at high speed and traps **insect prey** on its sticky tip!

The tiger chameleon's green skin helps to **camouflage** it among trees.

Southern Africa

Many of the **endangered** animals in southern Africa live in **desert** and **grassland habitats**. People here are building farms, roads, and towns on much of the land.

In southern Africa there are large areas of deserts and grasslands.

Namib Desert

Kalahari Desert

Grassland

Dry Forest

Drakensberg Mountains

N
W E
S

People have destroyed nine-tenths of the plants that these tortoises eat.

The geometric tortoise munches plants with its beak-like mouth. Females dig holes in which to lay eggs and then cover the eggs with plants. These eggs can take eight months to hatch!

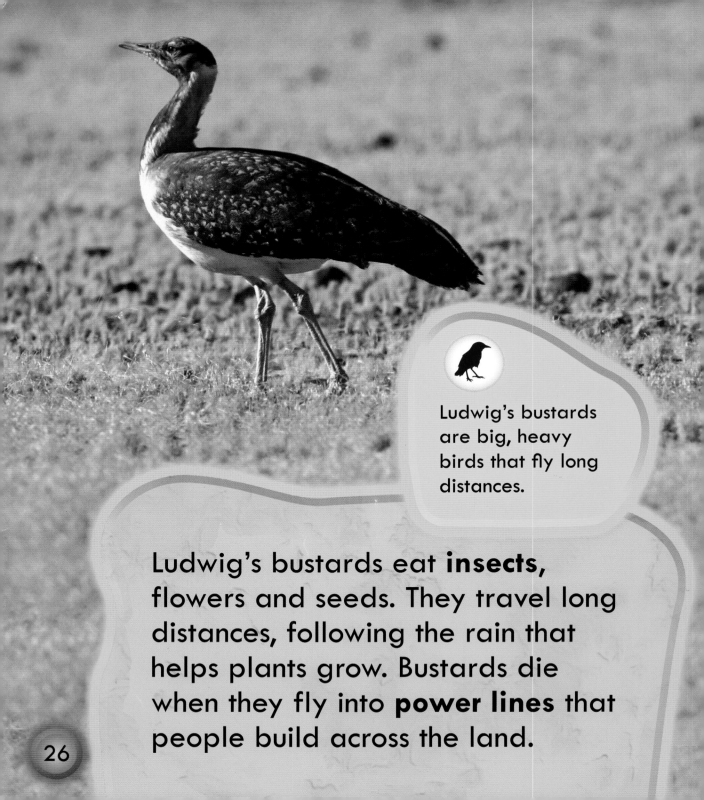

Ludwig's bustards are big, heavy birds that fly long distances.

Ludwig's bustards eat **insects**, flowers and seeds. They travel long distances, following the rain that helps plants grow. Bustards die when they fly into **power lines** that people build across the land.

The black rhinoceros has two horns. It uses these to fight off attackers, loosen soil in search of food, and break off twigs to eat. People kill rhinos and sell their horns to make medicine and ornaments.

Black rhinos are really gray in color.

Helping Africa's Animals

People help animals in Africa by making areas of land called **reserves,** where animals can live safely. People study animals in the reserves to check that they have enough space and food to survive.

Scientists study animals so that they can help them.

You can help **endangered** animals, too! You can find out more about problems facing wild animals and tell friends and family. You could raise money for **conservation** groups who help animals, too.

People support WWF because it protects endangered animals.

Glossary

camouflage color, shape, or pattern that helps an animal hide in its habitat

conservation protecting plants and animals

continent one of seven large areas that make up the world's land

desert hot, dry area of land often covered with sand and few plants

endangered when a type of animal is in danger of becoming extinct

extinct no longer alive; not seen in the wild for 50 years

fin flap of skin that helps a fish swim

global warming rise in Earth's temperature, probably caused by human activities

grassland area of land mainly covered in grass

graze to eat grass

habitat place where plants and animals live

insect small animal with six legs, such as an ant or fly

power lines wires that carry electricity to buildings

predator animal that catches and eats other animals for food

prey animal that gets caught and eaten by other animals

rain forest forest of very tall trees in hot, sunny, wet places

reserve large area of land where plants and animals are protected

scale small, overlapping pieces that cover an animal's body

webbed when feet have skin between the toes

wetland land covered in shallow water

Find Out More

Books

Haugen, Brenda. *African Elephants*. Mankato, Minn.: Capstone, 2012.

Kalman, Bobbie. *Why Do Animals Become Extinct?* New York: Crabtree Publishing Co., 2012.

Internet sites

Facthound offers a safe, fun way to find web sites related to this book. All the sites on Facthound have been researched by our staff.

Here's all you do:
Visit www.facthound.com
Type in this code: 9781432976729

Index